CONSERVATORY CANADA™

T0087373

New Millennium Voice Series

GRADE TWO

Editorial Committee
D.F. Cook
Elizabeth Parsons
Anita Ruthig

With thanks to Lisa Martin, Jennifer Floris, and Debra Wanless for their assistance.

Official Examination Repertoire List Pieces and Studies of Conservatory Canada - Grade 2

*Publication of the New Millennium Voice Series is made possible
by a generous grant from Dr. Don Wright.*

© 1999 Conservatory Canada
Published and Distributed by Novus Via Music Group Inc.
All Rights Reserved.

ISBN 978-0-88909-189-4

Novus Via Music Group Inc.
189 Douglas Street, Stratford, Ontario, Canada N5A 5P8
(519) 273-7520 www.NVmusicgroup.com

cover design:
Robin E. Cook, AOCA

About the Series

The *New Millennium Voice Series* is the official repertoire for Conservatory Canada examinations. This graded series, in eight volumes (Grade 1 to Grade 8), is designed not only to serve the needs of teachers and students for examinations, but it is also a valuable teaching resource and comprehensive anthology for any singer. The List Pieces have been carefully selected and edited, and represent repertoire from the Baroque, Classical, Romantic/Impressionist, and 20th-century periods. In addition, each volume includes the syllabus requirements for the grade, a graded arrangement of *O Canada* (with words in English and French), and a Glossary containing a short biography of each composer. Conservatory Canada requires that at least one Canadian composition be performed in every examination. Composers working in Canada are well represented in the series. A small asterisk next to their name identifies them. Photographs of some Canadian composers are included with the biography.

Notes on Editing

Most composers in the Baroque and Classical periods included only sparse dynamic, articulation, tempo and other performance indications in their scores. Where we felt it necessary, we have added suggested markings. The *New Millennium Series* is not an Urtext edition. All editorial markings are intended to be helpful suggestions rather than a final authority. The choice of tempo is a matter of personal taste, technical ability, and appropriateness of style. Most of our suggested metronome markings are expressed within a range of tempi. In the 19th and 20th centuries, composers included more performance indications in their scores, and as a consequence, fewer editorial markings have been required.

No markings have been used to suggest phrasing and breathing. In accordance with Conservatory Canada's policy regarding redundant accidentals, we have followed the practice that a barline cancels accidentals. Unnecessary accidentals following the barline have been used only in exceptional circumstances.

Bearing in mind acceptable performance practices, you are free to use your own judgement, musicianship and imagination in changing any editorial marking, especially in the areas of dynamics, articulation, and phrasing.

Every effort has been made to identify the authorship of texts and translations. Where we have not been able to confirm that the authorship is generally accepted as being anonymous, we have used the term "unknown". In the matter

The pieces in the *New Millennium Series* have been chosen as an introduction to enjoyable repertoire that is fun to sing while, at the same time, helps to develop your technique and musicianship. We hope you will explore the broad variety of styles and periods represented in this book. It is important that you learn as many pieces as possible before deciding which ones you will sing in the examination.

London, Ontario
September 1999

The Conservatory Canada Voice Syllabus gives full details regarding examinations. Teachers, students, and parents are advised to consult the most recent Syllabus for current requirements, regulations, procedures and deadline for application.

GRADE 2 - Table of Contents

Indicates Canadian Composer

WOODLAND LULLABY

McKellar

*W. H. Anderson
(1882-1955)

Peacefully ♩ = 54 - 66

Sleep__ in thy for – est bed.

Where__ si – lent falls the tread On the nee – dles soft and deep__

Of_____ the pine. Rest__ in thy per – fect dream.

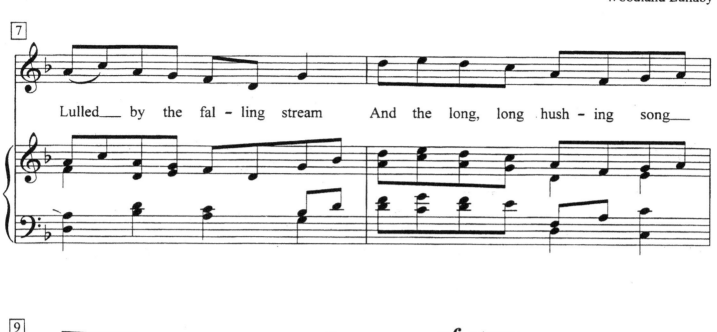

Lulled___ by the fal – ling stream   And the long, long hush – ing song___

Of___ the pine_____   Send__ might – y spir – it kind,

Send__ not the rush – ing wind,   Send a gen – tle slum – ber song___

Woodland Lullaby

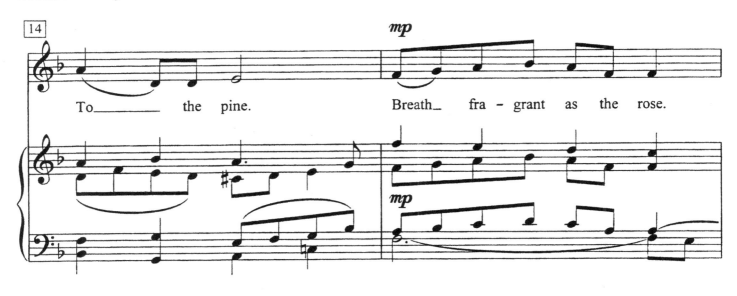

To_____ the pine. Breath_ fra - grant as the rose.

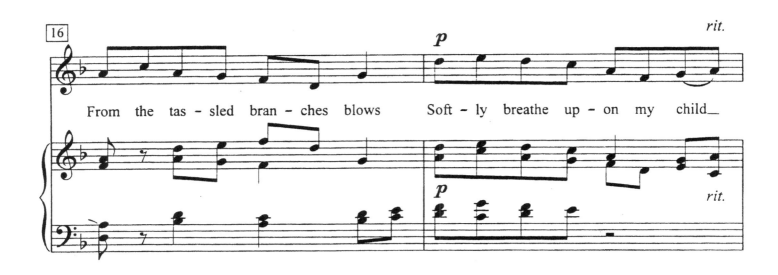

From the tas - sled bran - ches blows Soft - ly breathe up - on my child_

Moth - er pine._____

POPPING CORN

R. H. Greenville

*W. H. Anderson
(1882-1955)

The fire - light flick - ers, The

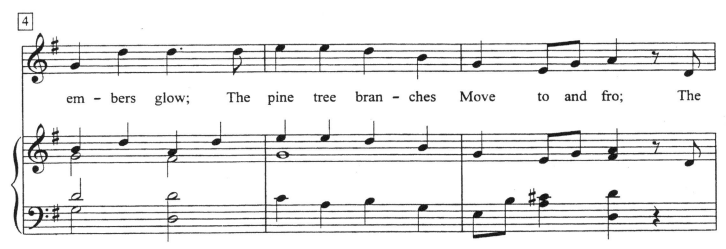

em - bers glow; The pine tree bran - ches Move to and fro; The

wind in the gar - den Sighs for - lorn, But we're in the par - lour,

Popping Corn

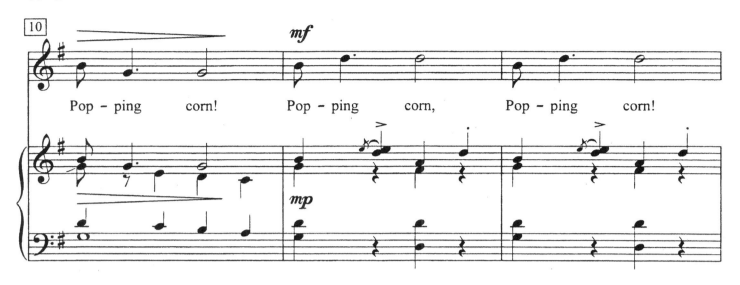

Pop - ping corn! Pop - ping corn, Pop - ping corn!

We're in the par - lour Pop - ping corn! Our

fa - ces tin - gle, Our cheeks grow red Like ripe fall ap - ples,

So dad - dy said. We laugh the chil - ly old winds_ to_ scorn,

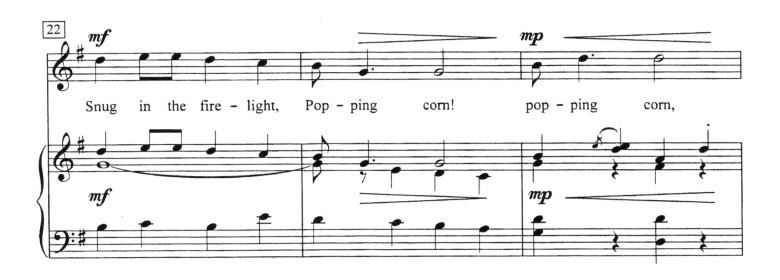

Snug in the fire - light, Pop - ping corn! pop - ping corn,

Pop - ping corn! Snug in the fire - light Pop - ping corn!_

THE NORTH WIND DOTH BLOW

Anonymous

*John Beckwith
(1927-   )

Andante ♩ = 88 - 104

The north wind doth blow, And we shall have snow, And what will the rob-in do then, Poor thing? And what will the rob-in do

8

AUTUMN

Dean Blair

*Dean Blair
(1932-   )

Expressive ♪ = 112 - 126

1. Ov - er - head   I
2. Gar - den flow'rs have
3. Soon the snow will

hear them call - ing,   From   the   cold,   clear au - tumn sky,
lost their pe - tals,   Col - oured leaves   put   on   a   show,
co - ver all the land,   And   the   winds   blow drifts so   tall;

Ducks   and   geese   fly   south   for   win - ter   Days   grow   short   and
Au - tumn winds   blow From   the   moun - tains   And   their   peaks   are
Smoke will   curl   from Farm house   chim - neys;   Skates   and   sleds   are   stand

10

FIGURE SKATING

Dean Blair

*Dean Blair
(1932-   )

Rhythmically, but with grace ♩. = 84 - 92

mf

mp

4

mf

North   winds   and   cold   have   now   froz – en   the   lake.
When   the   wind's   chill   I   go   stand   by   the   fire.
Oh   but   it's   fun   do – ing   fig – ures   on   ice.

mp

7

Skates   from   the   clos – et   I   hur – ry   to   take.
Of – ten   I   day – dream   my   great – est   de – sire.
E – ven   though   some – times   I'll   fall   once   or   twice,

10

Clear win - ter sky with the sun shin - ing bright.
Wait - ing my turn in a con - test some - day.
I keep on skat - ing un - til I must go.

To coda after verse 3

13

On such a day___ my dreams take flight.
Hear - ing the crowd cheer me all the way.
Then I'll walk home a - gain

To coda after verse 3

16 *mp dolce*

Glid - ing and turn - ing I skate light - ly and grace - ful - ly

p

Figure Skating

while   all   the   world   flash – es   by   quick – ly and   eas – i – ly.

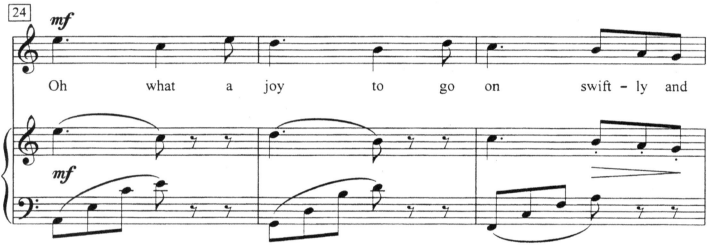

Oh   what   a   joy   to   go   on   swift – ly   and

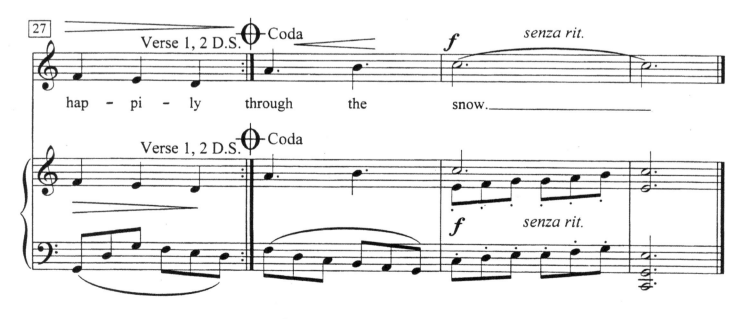

hap – pi – ly   through   the   snow.

14

THE KELLIGREWS' SOIREE

Johnny Burke

*Johnny Burke
(1851-1930)
arr. Mark Payne

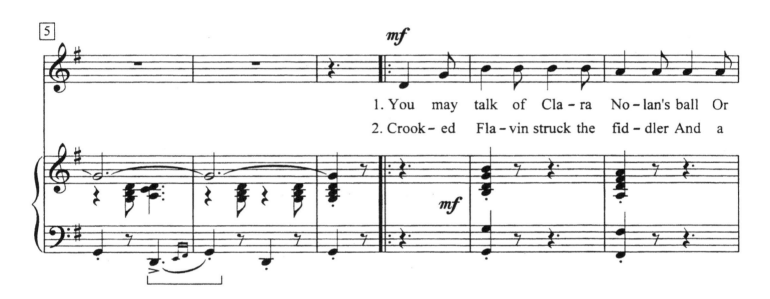

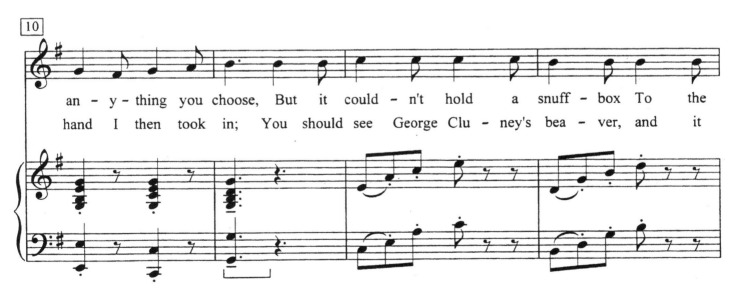

Kelligrews is a community in Conception Bay, Newfoundland, just outside St. Johns.
Beaver = a type of hat
Crackie = a small dog with a loud bark

tur-pen-tine, Jowls and cav - a - lan - ces, gin - ger beer and tea.

Pig's feet, cat's meat, dump - lings boil'd up in a sheet, Dan - de - lion and

crack - ies' teeth at the Kell - i - grew's Soir - ee.

PELICANS

Clifford Crawley

*Clifford Crawley
(1929-   )

1. The el - e - gant pe - li - cans
2. They wad - dle a - long on the

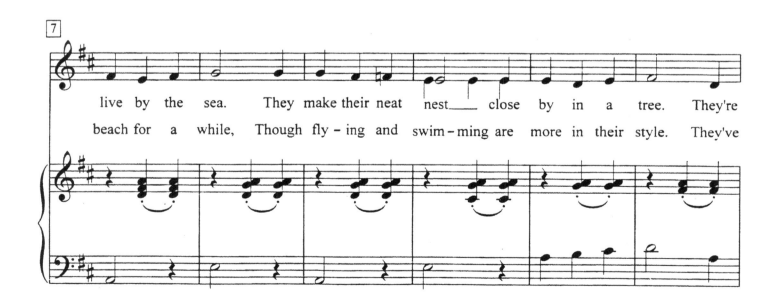

live by the sea. They make their neat nest___ close by in a tree. They're
beach for a while, Though fly - ing and swim - ming are more in their style. They've

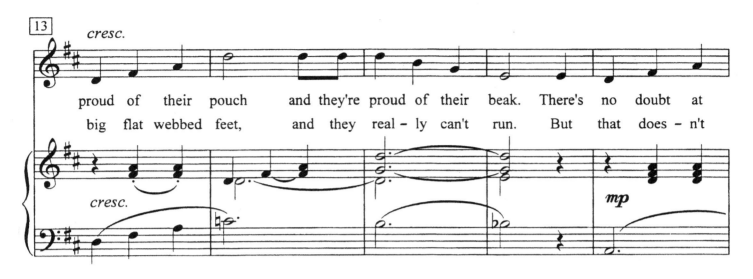

proud of their pouch   and they're proud of their beak.   There's no doubt at
big flat webbed feet,   and they real – ly can't run.   But that does – n't

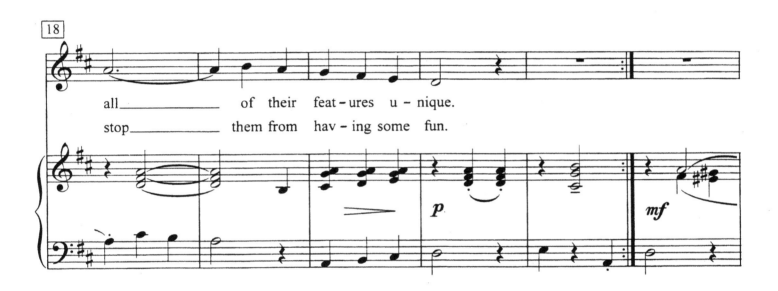

all_____ of their feat – ures u – nique.
stop_____ them from hav – ing some fun.

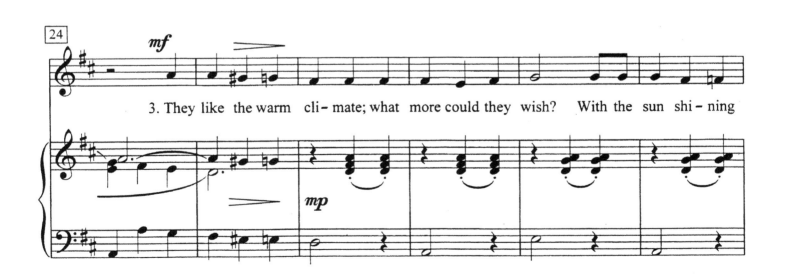

3. They like the warm cli – mate; what more could they wish?   With the sun shi – ning

Pelicans

30

cresc.

bright – ly and the sea full of fish. They fly high in the sky, then with whoosh and with

36

mf meno mosso

whish_____ Swoop down to sea lev – el to catch a

f veloce
3 3 3
ff
mf

41

sotto voce

fish (For fish is their fav – our – ite dish)

ppp
sfz

46

mf
a tempo

They're al – ways good

p
poco a
mf poco a tempo

A COUNTRY WALK

Kathleen Boland

*Clifford Curwin
(1929-   )

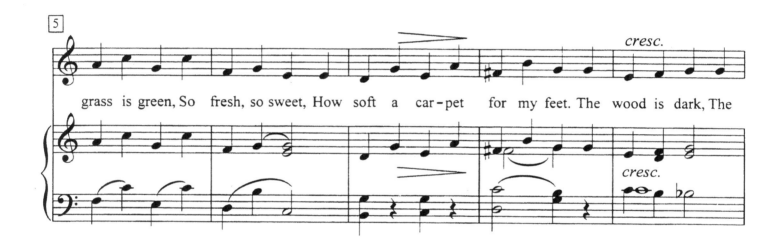

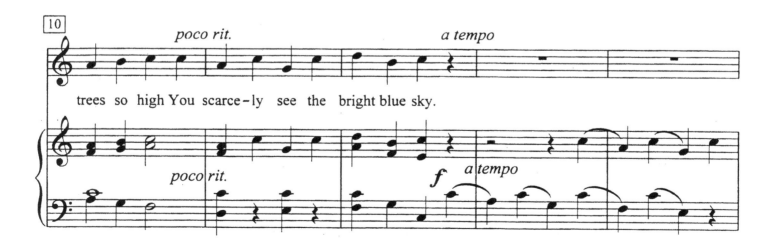

WE CAN MAKE A DIFFERENCE

Clifford Crawley

*Clifford Crawley
(1929-   )

1. We can make a dif – f'rence to this world we know and love. And
2. Let's pre – serve the good things, let us save the earth and sea. Get

keep it clean and whole – some so that stars that shine a – bove Can
rid of all pol – lu – tion, for on that we must a – gree. Or

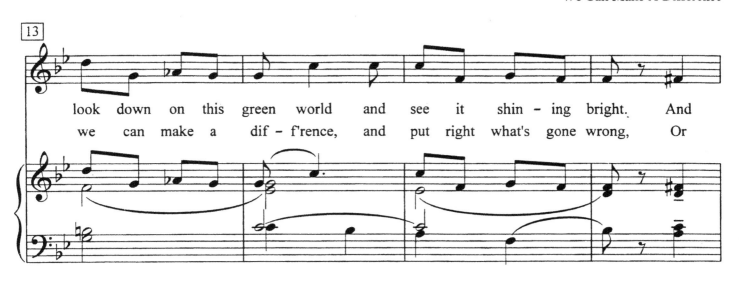

look down on this green world and see it shin - ing bright. And
we can make a dif - f'rence, and put right what's gone wrong, Or

say to one an - oth - er, "Ev - 'ry - thing's all right."

soon we'll find it's much too late. We dare not wait too long! So that

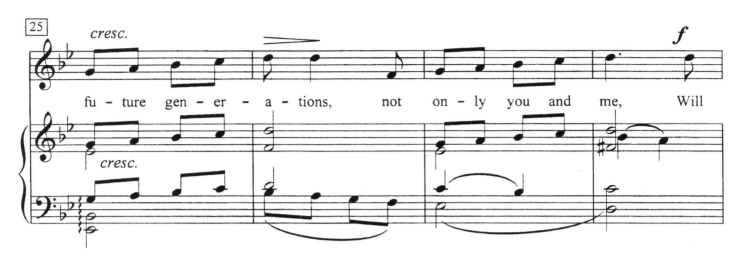

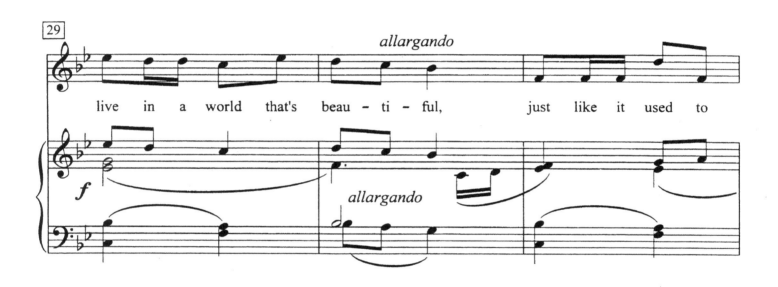

EVENING PRAYER

Sarah Wilson

Thomas F. Dunhill
(1877-1946)

Evening Prayer

What can harm me all the night?

Lit - tle lambs are calm - ly sleep - ing, 'Neath the o - pen

sky; In the shep - herds' watch - ful keep - ing Safe and warm they

THE FLOWER OF CHINA

H. W. Loomis

Chinese Melody
arr. D. F. Cook

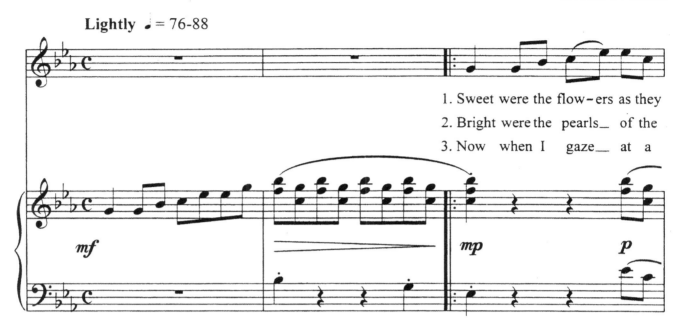

Lightly ♩ = 76-88

1. Sweet were the flow-ers as they
2. Bright were the pearls_ of the
3. Now when I gaze_ at a

hung on the vine,   Gay were the tunes_ that were sung on the vine;   Jas-mine stars on the
dew on the spray,   Soft was the breeze_ as he blew on the spray,   Bore the scent o - ver
star in the sky,   Gold in the gar - den a - far in the sky,   I shall dream of a

L.H.

green, green spray,   Bloomed for the birds at the dawn   of the day.

land and sea;   Here, with a song, he has brought   it to me.

jas – mine flow'r,   Waked by the birds in the down's   dew- y

hour.

SAINTE MARGUERITE

Traditional (Québec)
English version by unknown

*Canadian Folk Song
arr. W. H. Anderson

32

CHANUKAH, OY CHANUKAH

Traditional (Hebrew)

Hebrew Folksong
arr. D.F. Cook

Chanuka, oy Chanukah, a pretty holiday,
joyful and happy, there is none like it;
Every night we play with draydles,
eat steaming hot latkes without stopping.

Children quickly light thin candles,
tell about miracles.
Praise God for the miracles;
come quickly and dance in a circle.

SNOWFLAKE

Anonymous

*Cyril Hampshire
(1900-1963)

Daintily ♩ = 108-120

mf

I

watch'd a lit-tle snow – flake come dan-cing from the sky. It look'd at me a min-ute, And

fell right in my eye. A –

noth – er lit– tle snow–flake came dan–cing from the South, It looked at me a min–ute, Then

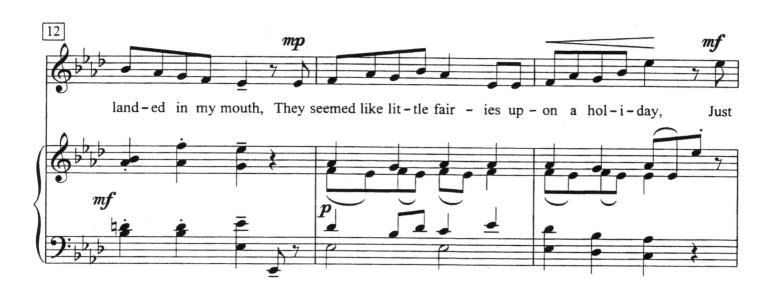

land–ed in my mouth, They seemed like lit–tle fair – ies up – on a hol–i–day, Just

out for fun a fro – lic, And ask – ing me to play.

poco rit.

BLOSSOM SNOW

Edythe Lever Hawes

*Burton Kurth
(1890-1977)

pet - als, Blown from the cher - ry tree,_____ They fall so white and

love - ly, A pret - ty sight to see._____ It's snow - ing, it's snow - ing

cher - ry blos - soms down._____

THE FROG

Nina Perry

Nina Perry
(1915-   )

Moderato ♩. = 69-80

mf

There was a Frog lived in a tree, Hum – ble – dum – dum, Hum – ble – dum – dee, He sat on a branch, and all day long

mp

mf

Puffed him – self up   and sang   a   song,

"Hum – ble – dum – dum,   Hum – ble – dum – dee,   I

wish   I   were   a   Bird",   sang   he.

And with a flour – ish he leapt from the tree.

"Now this is real – ly some – thing new, Hum – ble – dum – dum", he sang as he flew. But

The Frog

oh! this e – le – gant tal – ent – ed Frog Fin – ished up head o – ver

heels in a bog, "Hum – ble – dum – dum,

Hum – ble – dum – dee, The life of a Bird is not for me."

COLOURS

Christina Rosetti

Evelyn Sharpe
(20th Century)

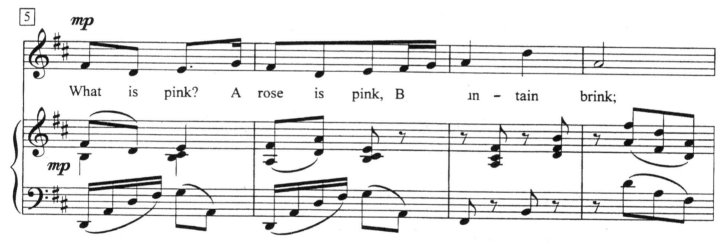

What is pink? A rose is pink, B ... n - tain brink;

What is red? A pop - py's red____ In its bar - ley bed.

Colours

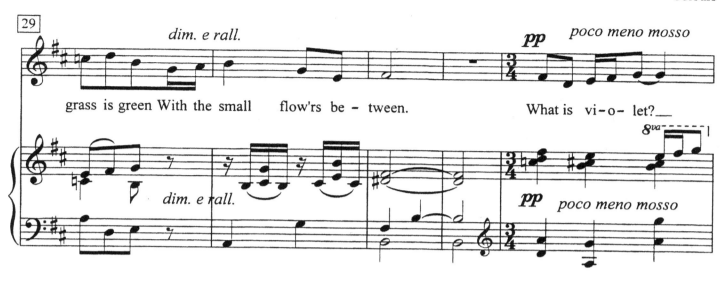

grass is green With the small flow'rs be - tween. What is vi-o- let?___

clouds are vi - o - let, In the sum - mer twi - light What is or - ange?

Why, an or - ange. Just an or - ange.____

THE CHERRY TREE

Doris Rowley

Alec Rowley
(1892-1958)

The lit – tle ro – sy cher – ry tree, Spreads

all its branch – es ov – er me, Its silk – y pet – als of – ten fall, And

drift in – to my ov – er – all.

THE FAIRY WEAVERS

Hilda M. Tharp

Alec Rowley
(1892-1958)

I'll tell you how the fair – ies have their

lit – tle dress – es made: They can – not man – age by them – selves with –

out the Spi – der's aid. For

Spi - ders have to spin the thread, and af - ter this is spun, The

weav - ing in - to fab - ric is by fai - ry fin - gers done.

The gol - den threads the fair - ies weave are rays from Fa - ther

Sun. The sil - ver threads are Moon - shine rays be - fore the day's be - gun.

The Fairy Weavers

The fab - ric then is fash - ioned by the

fai - ry tail - or Bee, Who makes them in - to dain - ty frocks for

Fai - ry Folks to see. They buy them from the

tail - or bee, and as they have no mo - ney, They pay him with the

52

rar - est kinds of lusc - ious flow - er - hon - ey. And

then the lit - tle Spi - der - folk must al - so have their pay, So

fai - ries find them mag - ic food to make them work___

a - way.

CHRISTMAS IS A FEELING

Natalie Sleeth

Natalie Sleeth
(1930-1992)

Moderato ♩ = 104-112

Christ - mas is a feel - ing fill - ing the air, it's

love and joy and laugh - ter of peo - ple ev - 'ry - where;

THE MIME

Roberta Stephen

*Roberta Stephen
(1931-   )

A mime is

si – lent.   Mak – ing stor – ies come a – live   with ges – tures

fun – ny – fa – ces   But   no words

Can you tell a stor-y with-out talk-ing or his-sing

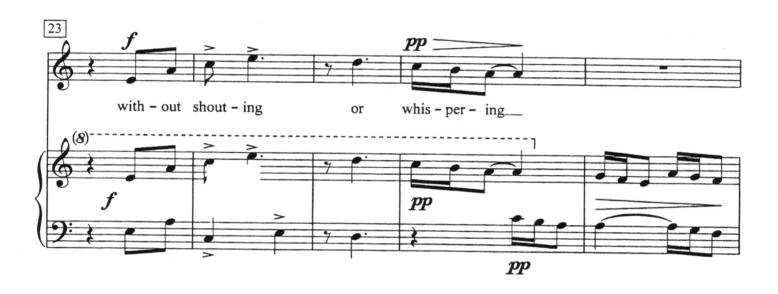

with - out shout - ing or whis-per - ing

Per - haps_____ with mus - - sic, mus - ic.

THE POOR SNAIL

J. M. Westrup

Harold H. Sykes
(died 1968)

Sadly, with expression ♩ = 58-66

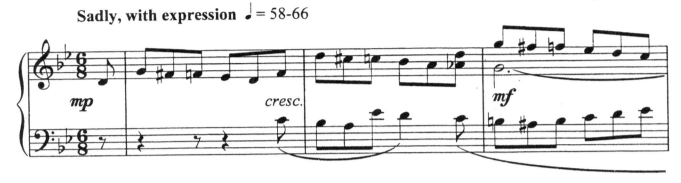

The snail says "A-las!" And the snail says "A-lack!" Why must I car-ry my

house on my back? You have a home to go in and out,

The Poor Snail

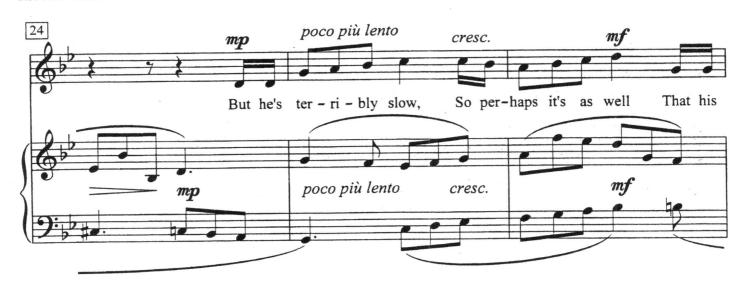

But he's ter-ri-bly slow, So per-haps it's as well That his

shell is his home, And his home_____ is his

shell.

GLOSSARY
Compiled by Debra Wanless

About the Composers in Grade Two

*ANDERSON, William Henry (1882-1955). Canada. Anderson was born in England, and studied in London where he sang in several church choirs and with an opera company. Chronic bronchitis ended his career as a vocal soloist, and he decided to seek a less humid climate. He emigrated to Canada in 1910, settling in Winnipeg, Manitoba where he worked as a voice teacher, choir director and composer. He composed more than 150 songs and approximately 40 church anthems.

*BECKWITH, John (born 1927). Canada. Beckwith was born in Victoria, British Columbia to musical parents who encouraged his talent. He began piano lessons at the age of 6 and as a young man, moved to Toronto in 1945 to study on a scholarship. He spent his entire life in Toronto, except for two years when he went to France to study composition with Nadia Boulanger. In Toronto he served as music critic, radio writer and broadcaster, professor and Dean of music at the University of Toronto. He composed operas and chamber music, as well as many pieces for orchestra, choir, solo piano and solo voice. His style is fresh and imaginative, and it has been said that he is the strongest voice among English-Canadian composers of our time.

*BLAIR, Dean (born 1932). Canada. Born in the US, Blair came to Canada as professor of composition at the University of Lethbridge. As a composer and performer he has appeared on television and radio. His works include piano, choral, percussion and vocal music.

*BURKE, Johnny (1851-1930). Canada. Burke was a Newfoundland poet and amateur musician, who fashioned some of his works after the popular Irish ballads of the 1890s. His work is included in the collection entitled *Old Time Songs and Poetry of Newfoundland*.

*COOK, Donald F. (born 1937). Canada. Donald Cook grew up and received his early musical training in St. John's, Newfoundland. After further studies in New York City and London, England, Dr. Cook returned to Newfoundland to become the founding director of the School of Music at Memorial University. Since 1992, he has served as Principal of Western Ontario Conservatory (now Conservatory Canada). Most of Dr.

Cook's compositions are for solo voice or choir, and many are based on Canadian folk songs.

*CRAWLEY, Clifford (born 1929).

 Canada. Born and educated in England, where he studied with composers Lennox Berkeley and Humphrey Searle, Crawley taught music in elementary and secondary schools before moving to Canada in 1973. He is a Professor Emeritus of Queen's University in Kingston, Ontario, where he taught from 1973 to 1993. He now resides in Toronto where he continues to compose and work as a music consultant, choir director, adjudicator, and examiner. Crawley has written more than 80 compositions, at times using the pen name Clifford Curwin. His works, many of which are intended for young players, include piano duets, operas, chamber works, and many pieces for band, orchestra and choir. Crawley is active in the "Creating Music in the Classroom" and "Artists in the Schools" programs in Ontario.

*CURWIN, Clifford. Pen name of **Clifford Crawley** (see above).

DUNHILL, Thomas Frederick (1877-1946). Britain. Dunhill grew up in London and received his musical training at the Royal College of Music. where he studied composition with Sir Charles Stanford. As a young man, Dunhill served as assistant music master at the famous boys' school, Eton College. He later taught at the Royal College of Music in London and spent more of his time composing. He wrote some chamber music, two light operas and two ballets. He wrote charming songs, many of them for children, and also children's cantatas, operettas, and other works intended for educational purposes.

*HAMPSHIRE, Cyril (1900-1963).

 Canada. Hampshire was a pianist, choir conductor, adjudicator and composer born in Wakefield, England. He was an assistant organist at the age of 14 and studied at Leeds College. Hampshire came to Canada in 1921 and lived for a time in Moose Jaw, Saskatchewan. In 1939, he became Principal of the Hamilton Conservatory of Music in Hamilton, Ontario. Six years later he accepted an appointment as director of music for the Hamilton public schools. It is therefore not surprising that he composed or arranged songs for school children, and also compiled the useful book *An Introduction to Practical Sight Singing*, published in 1951.

*KURTH, Burton (1890-1977).

 Canada. Kurth was a singer, educator, composer and organist who was born in Buffalo, New York. He studied in New York, Winnipeg and Chicago, settling in Winnipeg in 1909 to teach singing. He moved to Vancouver in 1927 where he had a long career as church organist and supervisor of music for Vancouver schools. Kurth

composed many songs for use in schools and compiled several collections including *Little Songs for Little People*, *Music Makers*, and *Sing Me a Song*. His book *Sensitive Singing* offers advice to young singers.

*PAYNE, Mark (born 1969). Canada.  Payne grew up in St. John's, Newfoundland and graduated with a degree in music from Memorial University of Newfoundland. Following further studies at the University of Toronto, he became a teacher and examiner at Conservatory Canada in London, Ontario. Payne performs in over 20 recitals each year, serves as a vocal coach at the University of Western Ontario and is sought after as a piano accompanist. His compositions are chiefly for solo voice or choir.

PERRY, Nina (born 1915). Britain. After touring Europe as a concert pianist, she returned to England and settled in Biddestone. She specialized in composing music for young people, and has written numerous children's pieces for choir, solo voice, and piano solo. Perry also composed a musical play based on the story of Puss n' Boots, called *The Marquis of Carabas*.

ROWLEY, Alec (1892-1958). Britain. Rowley was born in London and spent his entire career in that city. He studied at the Royal Academy of Music, winning prizes for both composition and piano. He was a fluent and original writer of songs, chamber music, and works for organ and piano. Much of his piano music is attractive and accessible to the young student.

SHARPE, Evelyn (20th century). Nothing is known about this composer.

SLEETH, Natalie (1930-1992). U.S.A. Sleeth was born in Evanston, Illinois and began piano lessons at the age of four. She studied at Wellesley College and Northwestern University. Sleeth worked as an organist and composed both sacred and secular choral works for all ages.

*STEPHEN, Roberta (born 1931).  Canada. Born in Calgary, Alberta, Roberta Stephen is a graduate of the University of Calgary and the University of North Texas. She now lives in Calgary where she is active as a teacher, composer, and adjudicator. Her music is performed across Canada and the United States. Stephen is also president of Alberta Keys Music Publishing Company.

SYKES, Harold H. (died 1968). Britain. Nothing else is known of this composer.

GRADE TWO – EXAMINATION REQUIREMENTS

Length of the examination: 20 minutes

Examination Fee: Please consult the current examination application form for the schedule of fees.

Co-requisite: None. There is NO written examination co-requisite for the awarding of the Grade 2 Practical Certificate.

NOTE: The Grade 2 examination is designed for younger singers. It is recommended that mature beginners enter the examination program at the Grade 4 level.

Candidates are expected to know all of the requirements and regulations for the examination as outlined in the current Conservatory Canada Voice Syllabus. In the event of a discrepancy between the current syllabus and the requirements set out below, the Syllabus must be considered definitive for examination purposes. No allowance can be made for candidates who misread or fail to follow any of the regulations and/or requirements for the examinations.

REQUIREMENTS & MARKING

Requirement	Total Marks
THREE CONTRASTING PIECES Chosen from the List (16 marks each)	48
ONE SUPPLEMENTARY PIECE	8
VOCALISES: None required	0
TECHNICAL TESTS	16

SIGHT READING
   Rhythm Pattern
   Singing
	
	3
	7

AURAL TESTS	10
VIVA VOCE	8
TOTAL POSSIBLE MARKS	100

NOTE: The examination program must include at least ONE piece by a Canadian composer. The Canadian piece may be chosen from the List Pieces OR as the Supplementary Piece.

PIECES
Candidates are required to perform THREE PIECES from the List, contrasting in key, tempo, mood, and subject. Your choices must include three different composers. All pieces must be sung from memory. Pieces may be transposed to suit the compass of the candidate's voice.

SUPPLEMENTARY PIECE
Candidates must be prepared to sing from memory ONE SUPPLEMENTARY PIECE. This piece need not be from the Syllabus list, and may be chosen entirely at the discretion of the teacher and student. It may represent a period or style of piece not already included in the examination program, but which holds special interest for the candidate. An unaccompanied folk song may be used. The choice must be within the following guidelines:

1) The equivalent level of difficulty of the piece may be at a higher level, providing it is within the technical and musical grasp of the candidate.

2) Pieces below the equivalent of Grade 1 level are not acceptable.

3) The piece must be suitable for the candidate's voice and age.

4) The piece must be for solo voice (with or without piano accompaniment). Vocal duets are not acceptable.

Special approval is not required for the Supplementary Piece. However, poor suitability of choice may be reflected in the mark.

TECHNICAL EXERCISES

Candidates must be prepared to sing any or all of the exercises given below, in the following manner:

i)   sung to the vowels

Ah [a], ay [e], ee [i], oh [o], oo [u]

as requested by the examiner.   Though the tonic sol-fa names may be used to learn these exercises, candidates may NOT sing using sol-fa names in the examination.

ii)   sung without accompaniment. A starting pitch will be given by the examiner. Exercises may be transposed from the keys given below into keys suitable to the candidate's voice range. The examiner may give a different starting pitch for each exercise.

iii)   metronome markings should be regarded as *minimum* speeds.

iv)   expression markings are not given for Grade 2 and are NOT required for the examination.

v)   all exercises must be sung in a single breath unless a breath mark is indicated in the score by a comma.

vi)   A slur has been used to indicate legato singing. Staccato markings have been used to indicate staccato singing.

SIGHT READING

Candidates are required to perform at sight a) a rhythmic exercise and b) a passage of vocal score as described below. The candidate will be given a brief period to scan the score before beginning to sing. However, Candidates are not permitted to hum the melody while scanning. Candidates must perform the rhythm section without counting aloud.   It is recommended that candidates maintain a steady beat, and avoid the unnecessary repetition caused by attempting to correct errors during the performance.

Before the candidate attempts to sing the vocal passage, the Examiner will play on the piano a I-IV-V-I chord progression (with the leading-note to tonic in the upper part) to establish the key and tonality. The tonic note will then be given.

a) *Rhythm*	b) *Vocal Passage*

To tap, clap or play on one note (at the candidate's choice) a simple rhythm.
 	
    Length   4 bars
    Time signature   3/4, 4/4
    Note values   1/2, dotted 1/2, 1/4, 1/8, &
                      dotted 1/4 followed by 1/8
    Rest values   whole, 1/2, 1/4
	To sing at sight a simple unaccompanied melody, within a range of six notes (*doh* to *la*) and within the limits of the great (or grand) staff. The melody begins on the tonic note. Candidates may use either any vowel of their choice or the tonic sol-fa names.
	    Major keys only C, F, G, D
	    Length 4 bars
	    Time signature 2/4, 3/4, 4/4
	    Note values 1/2, dotted 1/2, 1/4
	    Rest values whole, 1/2
	    Melodic Intervals 2nds and 3rds only

Example: a) Rhythm

Example: b) Vocal Passage

AURAL TESTS

The candidate will be required:

i)   to clap back the rhythmic pattern of a short melody in 3/4 or 4/4 time, consisting of half, dotted half, quarter, dotted quarter and eighth notes, after it has been played twice by the Examiner at the keyboard. Following is the approximate level of difficulty:

ii) to identify *major* or *minor* triad chords played once by the Examiner in broken form and in close, root position.

iii) to identify *major* or *harmonic minor* scales played once by the Examiner, ascending and descending, at a moderately slow tempo.

iv) the *major* common [four-note] chord of any key will be played once by the Examiner in broken form slowly, ascending and descending. The chord will be in root position. One of the four notes will then be re-sounded for the candidate to identify,by saying, at the candidate's choice:
    EITHER its interval number [1, 3, 5, 8],   OR its tonic sol-fa name [doh, me, soh, upper doh].

VIVA VOCE

Candidates must be prepared to give verbal answers to questions on the THREE List pieces selected for the examination. Candidates must ensure that all teaching notes and other written comments are removed from the score before the examination. The questions will include the following elements:

i)   to find and explain all of the signs (including clefs, time signatures, key signatures, accidentals, etc.), articulation markings (legato, staccato, accents, phrase or slur markings, etc.), dynamic and tempo markings, and other musical terms as they may be found in the three selected pieces.

ii) without reference to the score, to give the title, key and composer of the piece.

iii) to explain the meaning of the title of the piece.

iv) to find and play on the piano, any white or black note *within two octaves above or below middle C*, as requested by the Examiner. Candidates will NOT be required to read this note from score.

This page intentionally left blank
to facilitate page turns.

O CANADA

Written in French by Adolphe-Basile Routhier (1839-1920) in Quebec City and first performed there in 1880 to a musical setting by Calixa Lavallée. Translated into English in 1908 by Robert Stanley Wier (1856-1926). Approved as Canada's national anthem by the Parliament of Canada in 1967 and adopted officially in 1980.

Adolphe-Basile Routhier
English version by Robert Stanley Wier

*Calixa Lavallée
(1842-1891)
arr. D.F. Cook